Pain Won't Change My Mind

Nina Nero

Copyright © 2020 by Nina Nero.

Printed in the United States of America

ISBN: 978-1-63649-070-0

3

Dedication

I dedicate this book to Bishop Brian Fryer and the entire Fryer family.

Foreword

This book will help you understand that pain comes in different ways and that it has different meanings. Is there such a thing as good pain versus bad pain? Does pain have a purpose? These are questions that will be answered for you in this book. Romans 8:28 will become a reality and a clear and precise direction.

We thank God for Prophetess Nina Nero's transparency regarding her life and her life's pains and willingness to help so many people who deal with pain on a daily basis, pain that's unbearable and pain that life's threatening. Whatever pain you're dealing with, this book will give you insight and foresight.

Ask yourself the questions as you read this book to get the answers to the questions. Is pain permanent? Does pain really hurt? And does pain heal? Life is filled with pain of all kinds. But it's your decision on how to deal with pain.

Let's read together and get the answers to our pain questions. Be prepared to expect and receive with conviction. I'm so proud of our writer, Prophetess Nina Nero. May God's blessings be upon you and I pray that this book reaches and blesses many lives.

Continued blessings,

Bishop Keith Farmer

Chapter One

In 1999, I first experienced the death of my son. He was born on January 6, and he died at birth. I noticed that because of my drug addiction and not having a lot of prenatal care, he was unable to live. His death became my spiritual life. As I began to receive the baptism of the Holy Spirit in the hospital, days after he was born, I recognized that the spirit of pain. The tragedy demon was attached to me from that moment on. Ever since, I've had to experience one tragic event after the other. I've noticed that a tragedy attached itself to my life and I believe that it's because God understood that I was able to handle so many disappointing moments. I was married for the first time in 1989 and that marriage only lasted about a year or two. I was married to a drug lord who got our house shot up and he later ended up killing five people. He went to prison for the rest of his life. I was able to link up with Bishop Brian Fryer and we were married for about 30 years, this year. During our marriage, we suffered many events of pain. Pain became a part of our everyday regimen.

Sometimes, we had no food to eat and our bills weren't paid because there were times where he didn't work. I would have to go out and hustle just to make sure we could eat. There were so many times after my girls were born that I had to go out and go through other people's garbage just to fill up our house with furniture. My oldest was born in 1991. I would have to go into the rich neighborhoods and get carpeting, chairs and tables in order to have furniture in our house. I remember during a season of our lives when my husband was working at a laundromat called Marathon Laundry and he had two children prior to us being married and child support began taking all of his checks. When they started taking his check, he couldn't go back to work anymore because he would come home with $40 or $50 from working all week long and we had nothing. We were struggling. I remember that our house would get broken into and people would break into our cars and all of this time, we were still saved. We were still walking with God and believing and trusting God. We were part of my father's ministry at Landmark Temple of Deliverance and my husband and I were young ministers. We were coming up in the church and trying to keep smiles on our faces and trying to keep the illusion alive, but yet at home, we were struggling. We were living in the dark because our lights and gas had been cut off because of non-payment. So many times, my father would have to come to our rescue and take care of our bills because we were unable. I remember the times when I would seek the Lord and pray and ask God for a time of relief, but it seemed like relief never came. It seemed like all we were doing was suffering and I began to ask God if I was assigned to suffering because all of my life, I had to suffer from one level of pain to another.

Chapter Two

After the birth of my second child, my husband began working as a barber at a barbershop. God gave us a financial turnaround and life began to get a little better. But, I remember how every time we would take one step forward, it seemed like the pain of life would just push us back. We owned our home and we had tenants that lived there as well. It was a three-family flat, and it was as if we started to do a little better, but he and I would fight over crazy things. We would argue and it was always a time where pain was introduced into our marriage into our world. I used to say to myself, "pain will not change my mind, I'm not going to allow what I'm going through to change me from being the woman that God promised I would be."

I knew that I would be a great prophet, and I knew that I would be a great preacher because my father prophesied it to me. My mother prophesied it to me. While I was laying on my death bed having my son, my mother came to me and she said, "Nina, pray and ask God to spare your life." I told my mother, "Mama, God doesn't want anybody like me! I'm a drug addict. I'm a prostitute. I'm a liar. I cheat. I steal. I write bad checks. I steal people's credit cards. God doesn't want anybody that operates that way." She said to me, "If you ask God for your life... I'll tell you what, don't ask God for your life, but ask Him to save that ministry on the inside of you." I remember seeing my mother leave my bedside when the doctors told her that they didn't know if they could save me. My mother walked away and she went into the bathroom. She told me this after the event was over, she said, "Nina, I went in there and I got on my knees and I began to say to God, 'I don't care if you save my daughter, but save that ministry on the inside" and because of her saying that to God, He spared my life. Even though God took my son, my life was spared and I tell you today that in the midst of all of that pain, my mind never changed.

I never understood it, but down the road, I was able to see how God has used me through the pain that I have endured. He has used me to change lives and to help thousands of women all across the country. The pain won't change my mind. Everything that I began to endure as a young woman, from being raped, sodomized, abused, dragged down the street, tied to a car, thrown out of windows, shot in the arm... all that the pain that I have endured was so I can change lives from it. I can invest in other young women who are on the same road that I was on trying to find love, happiness and fulfillment and ended up in another segment of pain, but pain won't change my mind.

Chapter Three

I realized that the pain that has been assigned to my life had been assigned not to bring me down, but to bring me up. In order for people to understand how God will free you and how He will bring you back from a place of destitute and how He will bring you back from the edge, you must experience the pain, but yet, not let the pain change your mind. Once I was around the age of 26-27, I began to experience nauseating feeling in my stomach. I didn't understand that I was bulimic for so many years. I was anorexic because the pain would cause me not to eat, but to allow me to stay high all of the time, to allow men to abuse my body, to walk into prostitution, not understanding that the repercussions of prostitution would become everlasting. I remember a time when all I did was medicate the pain with every type of drug that I could get into my body, whether it was marijuana, cocaine, alcohol and any type of pill, just so that I could relieve the pain. When I was getting high, I thought I was experiencing life on another level, but I was actually trying to hide from myself. I was trying to hide from the pain that I had endured all my life, even as a little girl. I was rejected by my mother and father because I was different from all the rest of their kids. I didn't understand why I had to be the one that always was in trouble, always getting punished because I just would not follow the rules. The pain that I had suffered at 12 years old, being raped and sodomized by one of my father's deacons and them not believing me, turned me into a monster. But it never changed my mind. I had to understand that the pain that I had experienced is so much like the story of Job. I have gone through so many days of discomfort and so many days of my body not functioning properly. I don't know why God has allowed me to live this long with all of the physical abuse I have endured in this body. I have had pain at every level, but I will not let pain change my mind.

I remember when I was about 28 years old and I was pregnant by another one of the men I was involved with. When he discovered that I was going to have a baby, he picked me up and threw me out of a three-story window. I landed flat on the top of a car that was at the bottom of the apartment window. I got up and took off running as he started shooting at me because he was disappointed that I had allowed myself to get impregnated. I ran about three miles to my mom's house. I want to explain to you that the pain that I have endured has been life-long. I went to my mom's house and stayed there for about three weeks hiding out. Around the 4th week, I could smell something coming out of my body that was very foul and I didn't understand what it was. Unbeknownst to me, the baby had been crushed on the inside of me and while I was running, it started to break apart. I was living with a dead baby on the inside of my body for at least 4 weeks, but I did not let pain change my mind. I sat in the bathroom and they gave me some type of pill in order to induce labor.

The baby came out in the toilet, and I could pick it up because I might have been about 4 to 5 months pregnant. I was able to pick it up and look at the baby and say this is another segment of pain. This is another time in my life that I have had to endure the death of a child. I put the baby in a bag, took it out in my mother's backyard and buried it. The whole time, I was crying and asking myself why I allowed myself to keep going through this pain when God was calling my name? But pain didn't change my mind. I experienced so much pain in my young years that I felt like I was a tragedy attractor. I felt like tragedy saw me at birth and attached itself to me and refused to let me go.

Growing up, I was the middle child. I had two older siblings and two younger siblings and because I was hyperactive and socially awkward, taller than everyone else in my family, wilder and louder, it was difficult for my mother and father to connect to me in a way that a lot of mothers and fathers do. My mother and father were pastors and they always had to take care of sheep. Because of that, I was always getting into some type of trouble because I was an attention seeker. When you are the middle child, you try to find areas in your life where people pay attention to you. It was difficult for my parents, so they rejected me most of the time. I was always the only one who screamed at, the only one whipped, the only one that had to experience rejection on every level. I experienced rejection with my mother, my father, my sisters and my brother. It was difficult to grow up being the most rejected child in the family because it makes you question what you did to disappoint them so greatly? So, the pain that I endured as a young girl was greater than most people's because they loved me, but I don't think they liked me very much. The pain that I endured all of my life stemmed from my parents, not knowing how to care for me or love me the way that I needed it. So, because of that, it was difficult for them to receive a lot of the things that I said or did.

As I was growing up, I was very rebellious. I was always into stuff, always in the streets finding ways to disappoint them and that pain lingered all the way into my adult life. I sought so many different men and so many different relationships just trying to get attention and that attention demon that followed my life has caused me so much pain. But I will not let pain change my mind. I remember the first occasion when I was 17 and had gotten pregnant by one of the young men that I was dating. One of my good friends, Rose Corasco, took me to the Crenshaw District in LA and I got an abortion. When I got the abortion, it disappointed my mother so bad that she stopped talking to me for months. I didn't understand how a parent could go without saying a word to their child for months. My parents didn't know about it until after I had gotten back. I had mentioned it to one of my sisters and they told our parents. It was disappointing to them and from that point on, it seemed like my whole life just disappointed them, one event after the other.

I learned that the pain that I was experiencing from them was because of the pain that I put on them. I am at a place right now where I am experiencing pain at such a deep level that it causes me to always put other people through a certain level of pain. What I have done with this level of pain, through all of my adult life was take people for granted.

Chapter Four

I would misuse them, abuse them, manipulate them, rob them, rape men, hold them up at a gunpoint, rob banks and everything I could do to cause the same level of pain that I was experiencing on other people. I would be in relationships throughout my whole marriage. I always cheated and thank God for my husband taking me back the second time because our whole marriage, the first 28 years, I was never faithful. I wasn't faithful because I was so busy trying to inflict pain. I thought pain was pleasure. I thought pain was what made me complete and I didn't understand that I was hurting everything and everybody around me. I projected so much pain on Brian David Fryer that he would cry and beg me, "Please, stop it. If you would just stop it, we could still be together. We could still make it, but I just need you to stop." I would say to him, "I don't know how to stop." There was such an addiction for being unfaithful and an addiction for hurting people that I had to find somebody that I could manipulate and use to let them feel the pain that I had felt. Here I was, hurting the very person that was supporting me, taking care of me. He had my back no matter what. I don't care how many times I would stay out late at night and have all kinds of different text messages coming in, he would just look away like he didn't know what was happening. I knew he knew. The pain I saw in his eyes, day after day, was coming from deep inside of me and I couldn't let pain change my mind.

I'm sort of like Job. Before I get out of one thing, I'm right back into something else. It seems like my life has been one complete tragic event after the other. Ever since I've been in the church, I've been able to live for God and do the work of God, but yet I've always been in an area of pain that I have not been able to shake. This is mostly because I have had so many painful memories and so many painful moments where they just keep piling on top of each other. But, pain won't change my mind. I am still encouraged and still strengthened.

When God began to talk to me about Job, He talked to me about how Satan was allowed to touch Job. It seemed like before one thing could finish being said to him, another person was coming to tell him that something else had transpired, from his cattle to his home and then his children. It all took a toll on Job to where he found himself in sackcloth and ashes just crying out to God. That is where I find myself most days. Most days, I suffer in pain because I don't understand why I have to endure so much. Today was a very hard day for me because I had to pick up my husband's ashes. I experienced pain from picking up his ashes, just trying to pick them up from the door because they would not allow me to come into the funeral home. They set them outside on a table. We had to pick them up and put them in the car as if they were throwing away trash. The way that made me feel was so lost, empty and so incomplete.

Once I started having children, the doctors told me that I would never have children again after my son died. There was so much damage done to my uterus and my womb that they said I would never carry children again. There were many times my husband and I lost children, just coming out into the toilet and being unable to sustain and hold babies in. I began to pray and ask God to help me to not have to go through so much more pain. It seemed like every couple of years, I would get impregnated and they would just come right out. I thank God that He has allowed me to have the two children that I was finally able to conceive and carry, Shekinah Glory Fryer and Halayeah Rejoice Fryer, because I had to go through so much. I had to go through so many different procedures on my body to try to get them to stay inside of me. The pain that I experienced just trying to become pregnant and have children was a lot for my husband. I have had so many more days of pain than I have ever had of joy. I have had so many more days of crying than I have ever had of being happy. I have learned not to let pain change my mind because even though life has thrown me so many lemons, I have had to turn around and make lemonade from all of the bad experiences. There have been so many bad days, weary nights, that I have laid and cried out.

I remember when I was pregnant with my son and I had to push a car up a hill in order to get it home. We were coming home from church late one night and the car just stopped on us. I was out pushing the car, seven months pregnant, not understanding that all of this was going to have an effect on my son's death later on. Later on, I had to experience so many different physical ailments from being out there pushing that car, my son suffered so greatly. I had to take a moment and just "woosah" in my life. I had decided I wasn't going back to church anymore. I didn't want to have anything to do with my parents anymore because they were Christians. My father was a pastor and had been all my life. But I couldn't do it anymore and one day, God told me, "I have anointed you to be able to go through as a lamb." I didn't understand what that meant at the time. He said to me, "Must Jesus bear the cross alone and the whole world go free." I just didn't understand what I did to deserve this kind of pain all the time. What did I do?

I was seeing a guy, a famous singer back in the day, and all of a sudden, I noticed that I didn't hear from him much anymore. He started calling me and reaching out less and less. A few months later, I discovered that a young lady I used to be friends with had been trying to see him and they were having a relationship. I just didn't understand why so much pain? But, I realized that pain wasn't going to change my mind. As I began to experience the loss of my husband the first time, when we were divorced, I noticed that going through the divorce made me feel empty and lost. It made me feel as if I had given up on life. It made me feel like a part of me was no longer with me and even though I never told him, while we were divorced for three years, every day of my life, I cried and suffered because I knew a part of me was no longer there. I knew I was supposed to be his wife. I knew I was supposed to stay with him, but I was tricked by the enemy to believe that there was an incompletion in my heart.

There was an emptiness in me and I was looking for something to fill it. I was looking for something to fulfill it. All of a sudden, I had to wake up one day and say, "God, this is not you." I was engaged to a whole different man who lived in Atlanta and bought me a house and a Mercedes. I thought God was blessing me, I was doing television and radio and I was moving forward. I was trying to progress in life and all of a sudden, I got a phone call on December 17, 2018. They told me that a bullet went through and into my daughter's head. This was happening along with all of the other things that I had already experienced in my life, along with my son dying, my marriage dying, our churches dying, now, my daughter had a bullet in her brain. This was a random shooting. It wasn't even a targeted shot. It was a random shot. Someone was shooting and it just hit her. I had to come to the realization that God was answering prayer. I felt like it was going to be the death of me to walk in that hospital room and see my daughter strapped down, tubes in every hole in her body, her head draining and dripping.

It took everything in me not to scream as loud as I could. When I finally got to the hospital, seeing her like that devastated my life. When there is nothing that you can do but watch the machines go up and down, watch the blood pressure get out of control and then level back down and listen to them say to you that there was nothing more they could do, I just had to wait. To have your child with a tube down her throat and stitches in her head was unbearable. They had to go into my daughter's head eight different times because of the bullet fragments moving. One time, right after the initial shooting, everything in her body was working, both of her legs, her arms and her muscles were working right, but she had a brain bleed and because the nurse wasn't watching her close enough. Her brain started to swell and blood began to form in her brain. Because of that, I had to watch her go into a coma and slip in and lose consciousness. They had to go inside of her head so many different times, eight different surgeries over the course of about 2-3 weeks. They had to continue to go back and forth inside of her head.

I couldn't leave the hospital. I didn't have anywhere to live because, at the time, I was living in Atlanta. I left Atlanta and came home to see about my child and I slept in the hospital. I slept on the floor next to her bed. I slept in the bathroom. I washed up in the bathroom. I was unable to take a shower because they didn't have facilities for that. I stayed there and watched the pain of my daughter's shooting permeate through our family to a place where people started coming from all over the country just to see about her. We had people flying and driving in from different parts of the country just to see about Shekinah Glory. I tell you, it was such a blessing, but the pain was excruciating because there was nothing anybody could say or do to make this thing feel better. Even though they were walking in that waiting room, person after person, sending money, food and clothes for me, none of that made the pain subside. Watching my child in agony with nothing that I could do was excruciating.

I remember when the doctor came in and told me that the drain stopped working because of the negligence of the nurse. They had to go back into my daughter's head and take a piece of her brain out. The piece they took out was her left side motor skills, so when she woke up this time, she couldn't move anything on her left side. The pain of seeing a young woman who was vibrant, no children, no husband, a praise and worship leader singing all over the country, become reduced to a paralytic person at 27 years old with no fault of her own was very hard. I can't even say she was at the wrong place at the wrong time because this shooting happened right in front of her own house. She pulled up from work, parked in her driveway and just sitting there. All of a sudden, here comes a bullet from nowhere and hits her in the head. The pain that is associated with watching your child try to live a fulfilled life as a half of a person is unbearable. She can't sing anymore. She can't walk anymore. She can't even go to the bathroom on her own anymore. Everything about her life has been destroyed and distorted because of one bullet, but I won't let one bullet change my mind.

I began to realize that this was a test. This was a test for our family because, at the time, my husband and I were divorced and had been divorced for almost 3 years, but this tragedy brought our family back together.

Chapter Five

We came back together and we got remarried on April 24, 2019. At the wedding, which was at her rehab, she came into the wedding with stitches going straight down her face and across her head because they had to take part of her skull off. Just to see her with half of her head gone and yet coming to the wedding and sitting there crying as she watched her father and I reunite. The pain that I had to endure, standing there saying, "I do" yet, looking at my daughter and I know she never will. I did not let that pain change my mind. As we began to progress in life, she went to rehab and I watched how they were working with her and teaching her how to walk, stand and use her left side. You can't even imagine what it feels like to watch your vibrant child, not even be able to sit up. She needed someone to prop her up and hold her up. She spent day after day looking at the bathroom and she used to say, "Mama, I just want to go to the bathroom. I just want to get up and go to the bathroom." People take such a small thing for granted. Her body would not cooperate, her body wouldn't move and I had to stand there and watch this and endure the pain with her. But I wouldn't let pain change my mind. When you get to a place where pain becomes a regimen of life, we have to begin to allow prayer to become our everyday interaction with God because you will get to a place where pain will subside, but you cannot let it change your mind.

I am glad that the shooting did not leave her disabled mentally and emotionally. Even though her body is not up to par, her mind is still strong. She is still happy and every day, we miss her father more and more. The shooting handicapped me emotionally and it put me in a place of being numb. The pain that was associated with her tragic incident no longer hurt once I came to terms with "all things work together for the good to them that love the Lord who are called according to His purpose." I know that everything that has transpired is from God and it is the will of God. Even if I am not in agreement with the pain that I have had to endure, I do know that it is because of God's mercy and God's grace that I have been able to endure without losing it. The whole year of 2019, after my daughter's shooting, she was in rehab, learning how to use her motor skills again. The difficult part of watching someone who was vibrant and alive, now unable to lift her arm or move the muscles in her fingers, is very difficult. You learn to take the pain and put it in perspective. You learn how to take the pain and put it into compartments, where you compartmentalize all of your disappointments and your brokenness so that the person you are suffering this pain from will not have a setback, based on your emotions. So many days, I watched her cry and wonder why this happened to her.

As a mother, a pastor and a prophetess, I was unable to give her any insight or speak to her in terms of why God allowed what He allowed to happen and not move her head one inch so that the bullet wouldn't touch her, as it did the neighbor or post office worker. When I went to find out how this incident occurred, they told me that both of them were standing outside when my daughter pulled up in the driveway and she was just sitting there, looking in their direction. The mailwoman said that she heard the bullet go past her. She heard a sound and directly after she heard it, she saw my daughter's window crash and she slumped over. If the mailwoman had been one inch up, or one inch back, the bullet that caught my daughter's head would have killed one of them. I just thank God that as we begin to embrace this new lifestyle that we are living, we have not had a moment of insanity, which is what I believe the enemy is trying to do to me now. It seems like every time I turn around, I am in a situation of pain, but I have learned that pain will not change my mind.

Chapter Six

After learning that she would be paralyzed, unless therapy would work, it was so difficult to know that I would have to endure knowing that I would have to help my daughter go to the bathroom daily. I would have to change her daily, sit her up daily, feed her, give her medicine daily. My husband was here to help me and to go through this with me. Even though mothers suffer and endure pain on different levels, it still was heartbreaking to know that there was nothing that I could do to bring some type of solution to her situation. Because of that, I had to say to myself every day, "pain will not change my mind."

I had been doing some research on the word "pain." One of the things that I have been able to investigate is that it is physical, suffering, distress, illness, injury, depression, and sensation. Pain is peculiar to parts of the body that you cannot even detect sometimes. It can be mental, emotional and tormenting. Pain has its own ability to create a world around you and you don't even realize how it can be a prison. If we are not careful, we will get trapped in the prison of pain, unable to escape. What happens is, the spirit of oppression and suppression will begin to sit in and overtake us, but we are in the prison of pain. If we are not careful, pain becomes suicidal. It becomes carefree and effortless.

Have you ever known people that spend their whole life talking about what they've been through? The pain that they have endured? The pain that they have suffered? How their mother or father treated them? How they have been molested? How they were mistreated or neglected? They spend so much time in pain that they forget that the joy of the Lord is our strength. They forget how to come out because they have been locked in the prison of pain. If we are not careful, pain will cause us to be nefarious and it will take the care away. The greater the pain, it will begin to take a toll that is almost unrepairable. When you are annoying or troublesome, it can cause physical pain and hurt. Emotional and mental hurt and depression stem from a pain that not only we have allowed to lock us into prison, but the pain that we refuse to come out of. If we feel pain, then we feel intoxicated. After all that we have endured, the toxicity of pain is almost so unbearable that it keeps you from being able to breathe. It keeps you from being able to live. Pain will push you into a depression and depression will put you into a suppression, which means that depression comes to depress you, suppress you. The next thing you know, you are in a deep place. In order for us to release ourselves from this pain, we have to stop it before it gets intoxicating, smothers us, or it overtakes us. That is what pain does. We cannot allow pain to change our minds.

The word "intoxication" came to me as I began to talk about how pain will almost handicap you. The effects of it are temporary, but it can affect the capacity of your physical and mental control. Addiction to pain is like being an alcoholic. When pain gets so deep in your life, you become addicted to the pain so much so that you need it to survive. We will begin to find ourselves in painful situations that we create for ourselves. One of the things that I have discovered in that is that people, just like when they need attention, sex or drugs, pain becomes a drug. We are addicted to being in a painful situation because it gets us attention. It gets us self-pity. It gets people to focus on us. It allows people to begin to sympathize with us and that can be addicting. Some will spend so many days waiting for someone to ask, "Are you okay?" "Is there anything I can do?" So, we adopt pain as a normal part of our lives, not understanding that this is not from God. It is not what God ordained for us to be in. We are not supposed to be in pain daily and be addicted and intoxicated as if we are alcoholics or drug-addicted people. It is really bad, especially when we become excited about how people treat us when they know we are in pain. Pain won't change my mind. One of the scriptures that was brought to mind concerning pain is Psalm 69:29 and it says, "I am hurt and in pain. Give me space for healing and mountain air." I do know that when you are in pain, you have to take a moment to step back and realize that this pain that you are in needs to be analyzed. You must see if it was a self-induced pain, pain brought on by bad choices and decisions, or pain that has been inflicted upon you because we don't have a "no" button. Sometimes, we don't have a "stop" button or a "pause" button. Even though life pushes us into areas where we need to seek God and we need to pray, some of the time, we are putting ourselves in positions that will create pain. When I cheated on my husband, I was creating pain, not only for me but for my whole family. What people don't understand, like how I didn't understand, is that pain is almost hereditary. Pain will go from person to person, situation to situation and instead of us learning how to deal with our own idiosyncrasies, our own failures and brokenness, we will cause other people to hurt because we don't know how not to hurt. When I began to read this scripture, I saw where it says the first thing is, I need space. Sometimes we have to take a moment and step back. I've had to stop, I brought myself out of the church, I brought myself out of the pulpit, even though we are unable to go into the pulpit at this time, we have our Zoom services every Sunday. I have brought myself back. I have brought myself down so that I can begin to reevaluate what God will have me to do. If this is God's plan for my life, I must step back because pain won't change my mind. I realized that hurt people hurt people. The more pain that I endure as a leader, I just begin to bleed all over the people because if you are hurting and laying hands, hurting and ministering, hurting and prophesying, then you are hurting the people and sheep that God has placed in your fold. He has placed these people under your care. He's made you a shepherd and even shepherds have to take a moment and go somewhere and reevaluate. Shepherds have to go somewhere and deal with the pain, process the pain and allow yourself time for healing. You must allow yourself time for God to mend you back together and because we don't take the time that we need, all wounds bleed. The more wounded you become, the more bloody you become. The more people we hurt day by day, we begin to give people pain by our sharp tongue, we give people pain by our brass attitude. Everything about our lives becomes so harsh and we don't even know how to deal with the sheep because of the pain that we are enduring. Because we are in so much pain, we take that out on people every day. We take it out on the store clerks, the bank teller or gas station attendant. Why? Because I am in pain and if I am in pain, I need to produce more pain for people all around me. We have to be careful, especially as leaders. Do not let pain change your mind. Instead, embrace that pain and go somewhere and get healed. Go somewhere and sit down, go and have several seats, so that God can speak to your heart. Go to the mountains, as the scripture is saying. You need space for healing. You need to take time out to deal with the pain. Take time out and face the pain. One of the things that I have done and I am doing is learning that the most important thing for me right now is to stay home.

I must deal with the loss, all of the losses I have experienced over the last 58 years. All of the pain that I have had to endure, I am dealing with it. I am in the mountain and buried inside of it because I need God to process this pain. I need Him to take this pain and allow me to be able to walk through the pain, walk with the pain and yet walk and be delivered from the pain. I don't want God to take the pain away. I want Him to teach me how to process it and take that p-a-i-n and break it down into words that will help me move the wall. We cannot let pain change our minds, but we have to take the intoxication of it and begin to walk free from it. We have to know that, especially if we are excited about our future, our futures are great. Our futures are phenomenal, and I know it is because the Bible says, "To whom much is given, much more is required." For what I've had to endure, what I've had to suffer, what I've had to live through, I know that there are great things coming after this.

There is greatness behind this pain. I want to take the pain and not let it change my mind, but process it and make it become phenomenal in my life. You can take the pain that you have endured as a child and process it and instead of becoming intoxicated by it, you can become great through it.

Made in the USA
Middletown, DE
25 September 2021